Esther

A Bible Rhyme book.

Words by Bard Art by Clicker

I0110975

<u>Esther:</u>
A Bible rhyme book.

Dedicated to Mum & Dad, Ann & Bill

A catalogue record for this book is available from the British Library.

ISBN: 978-0-9954770-0-1

Published by Lamb & Priestly

email: lambandpriestlypublishing@outlook.com

Font: 'Chronicles of 8 Hero'
(c) copyright Blambot comic fonts
http://blambot.com/

The palace stood in Shushan
Ahasuerus there was King.

The land lavished in prosperity
and didn't need a thing.

1

This Persian King loved feasting

and showing off his wife.

Her beauty was well-known but Vashti gave him strife.

2

One day the King invited all Shushan to a feast

Everyone could come from the greatest to the least!

Esther's parents both had died
& so her uncle was her guide.

Righteously they lived & prayed
they kept the Torah & obeyed.

The virgins were gathered in Shushan city
and all of them were very pretty!

Esther was bathed in myrrh and oil
which made her smell like something royal.

In and out the bath she'd climb
and this went on for quite a time.

When night fell as it always does
the palace was filled with quite a buzz!

It was Esther's turn to see the King,
She'd been chosen to go in.

11

With all humility in she went,
her gaze averted, her neck was bent.

but as soon as
Esther's gaze
was met
the wedding day
was quickly set!

He put the crown on Esther's head
so she was queen
in Vashti's stead.

So when the matter all was done
both the traitors swiftly hung.

Up 'til then it wasn't known
that Esther kept a kosher home!

14

But after Haman
got promotion
against all Jews
he caused commotion.

One day when Haman
was in the street
he ordered
the people
to bow at his feet.

But Mordecai faithful & Mordecai true
said that was a thing
he just wouldn't do.

Haman so seething and raging with hate

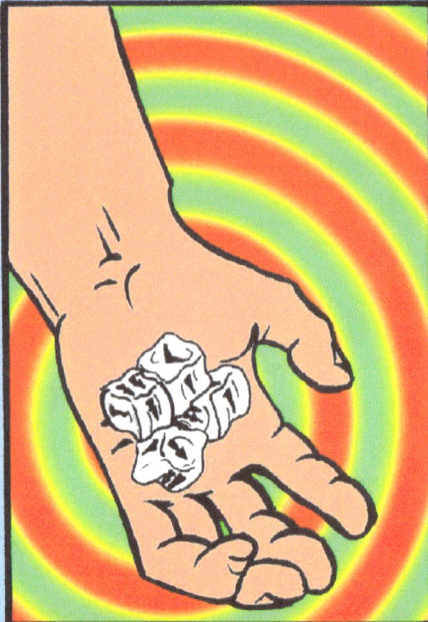

went to cast lots to seal the Jews fate!

He went to the King and told him a tale

that may have made his face turn pale.

16

A decree was written and royally sealed to which all peoples had to yield.

Letters were sent and orders deployed that all the Jews must be destroyed.

Adar The 13th on that evil day their lives and possessions taken away.

The couriers went by command of the King.

And Shushan city heard the thing.

The King and Haman sat and boozed...

...but all in Shushan were confused.

19

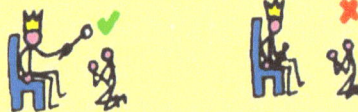

After three days
fast and prayer

The throne room
curtain was ajar,

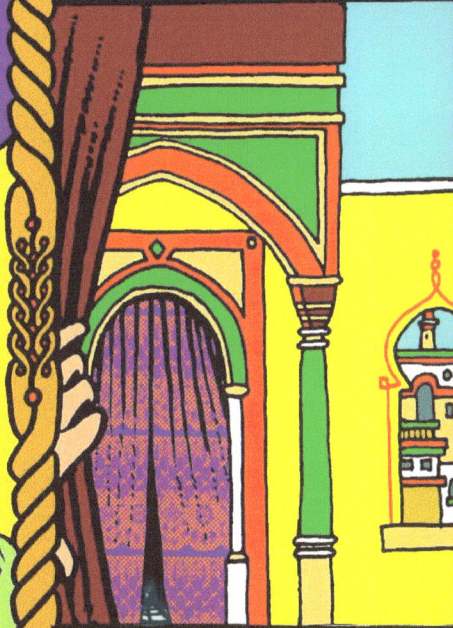

she determined
to go there.

So she trod
the journey far!

And to her joy,
oh raise a shout!

Her husband
held the
scepter out!

21

Haman went out
his heart was glad
but seeing Mordecai
made him mad.

Haman went home to his friends and his wife
and told them of his so blessed life.

23

The King then asked

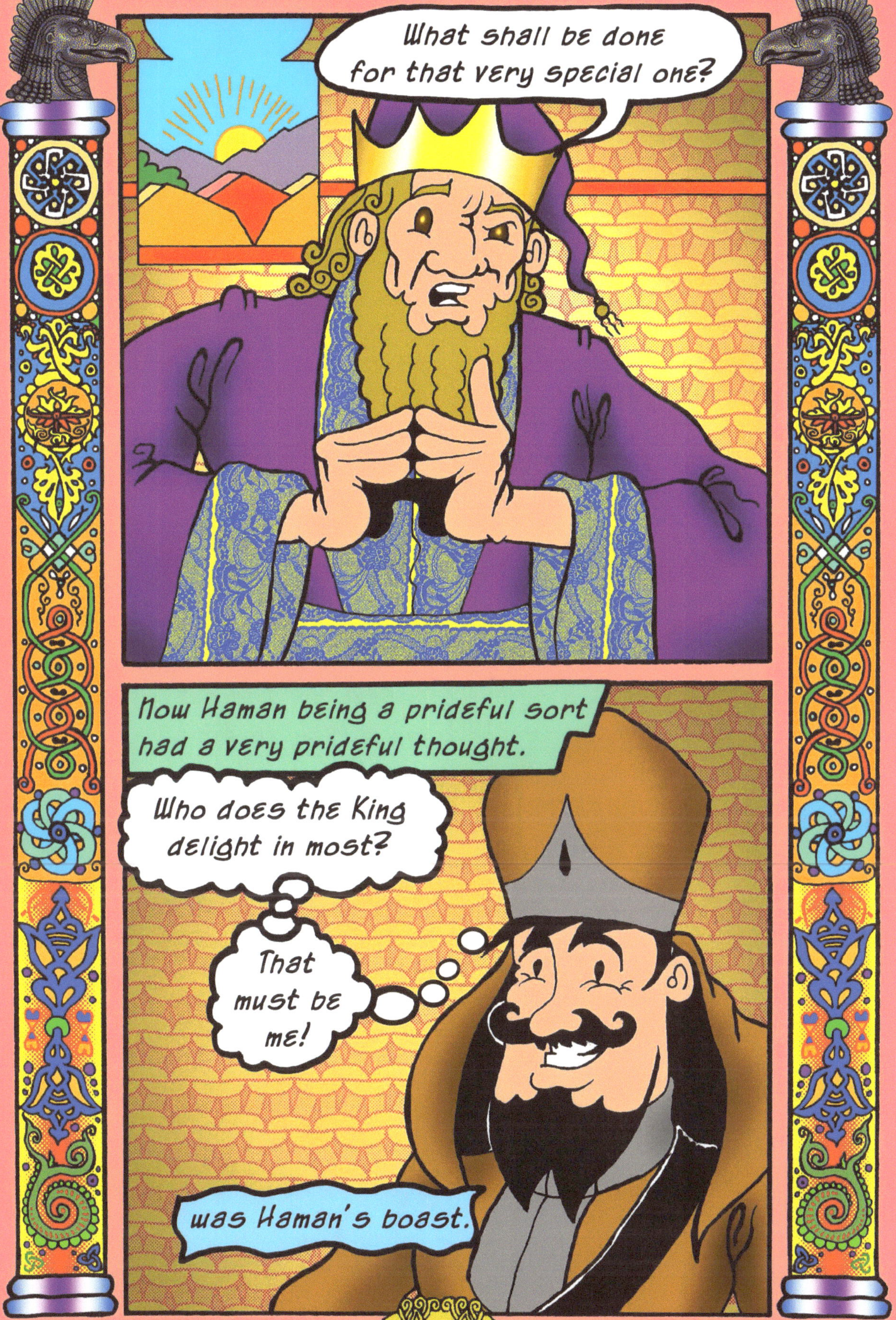

Haman went as he was bid and burned with anger as he did.

All the people heard him say that Mordecai was blessed today. He shouted loud ...

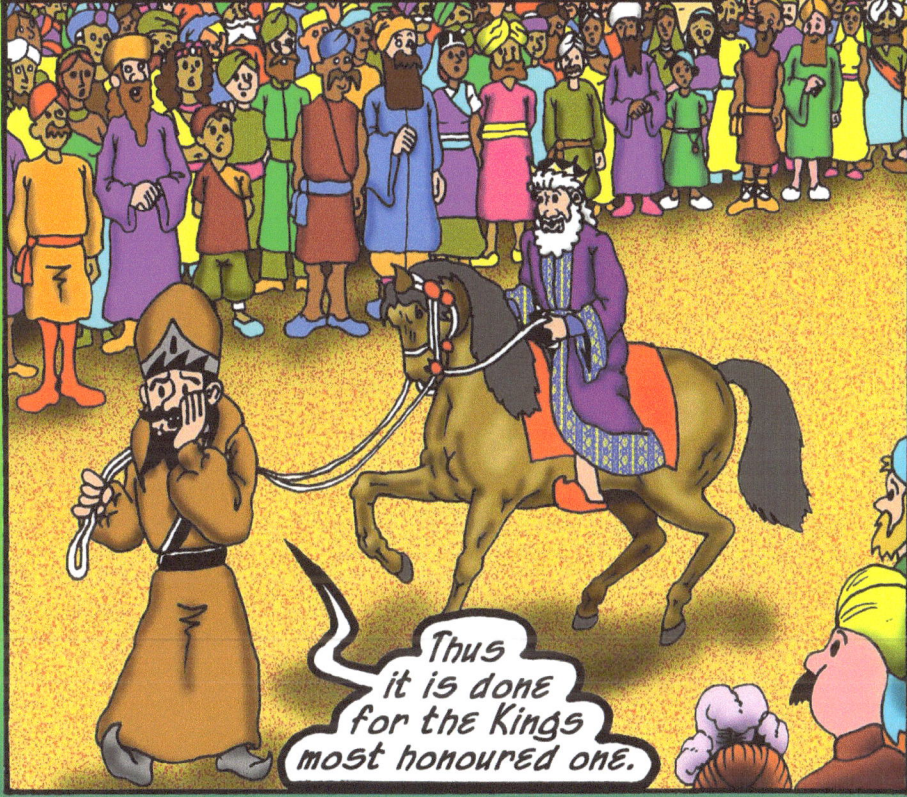

Thus it is done for the Kings most honoured one.

Mordecai blessed returned to his place

but Haman went home with shame on his face.

When the sun was set and the table too queen Esther gave a pleasing do!

Esther told the King with pain why she'd asked them there again.

Someone was trying to kill her clan and that someone was ...

this Haman!

30

Well in deep anger the King did leave
he found it all hard to believe!

Haman tried to change his fate
But Esther knew it was too late.

He tried to wipe her people out,
of that she knew there was no doubt!

31

As Esther reclined upon her seat Haman saw that he was beat.

So Haman fell face down by her

as the King came back

and cast his 'pur'!

The King in wrath and without sorrows ordered Haman to the gallows.

The story doesn't quite end yet but dear reader don't you fret! If you turn to Holy Writ you can read the rest of it!

Esther

Mordecai

The book of 'Esther' is named after its main character. She was a Jewess living in the Persian capital city of Shushan. The ruler at the time was King Ahasuerus who was also known as Xerxes.

'Esther' is a story about the rescue of the Jewish people from a tyrant named Haman. It contains, among other things, a beauty pageant, a murder plot, two big feasts and a wedding.

The story of Esther is the reason that the Jewish people celebrate the feast of 'Purim' where they dress up in colourful costumes, re-enact the story and eat cookies in the shape of Haman's hat remembering that GOD, who is not mentioned by name in the book, is always in our situations working for our best even when we're not aware of it.

In the story, Esther felt unsure of herself, but it soon became clear to her that she had a very special purpose and that purpose was to save her people.

GOD has a purpose and a plan for each one of us. We only need to ask Him to show us what that might be.

Ahasuerus

Haman

www.ingramcontent.com/pod-product-compliance
Lightning Source LLC
LaVergne TN
LVHW072057070426
835508LV00002B/148